Praise for *Italics*

"Where most poets want our attention, Alison Davis wants our participation. *Italics* is a map to wonder—motherhood, grief, desire, wilderness, and the daily work of staying human—drawn by a mind that's mastered curiosity and a heart that refuses to quit as we ponder together the biggest of questions: 'what to do with all this beholding?' The book left me feeling more grateful and slightly askew."

— Timothy Green, editor of *Rattle*

"Alison Davis' poems are healing, enlivening, seriously thought-provoking, and like a series of invitations to fully inhabit one's own life the way this poet inhabits hers. These are the poems of the constant seeker who also remembers that which is sought for is already found. 'We have to stop thinking we are in the wrong place,' one poem ends. This book is for you, seekers, and for all who appreciate beauty that shines a light, whether it be the light found in grief, in peace, or in the courage required to live with arms and heart and eyes wide open."

— Jane McCafferty, professor and author of *First You Try Everything*

"I love these poems. I love Alison Davis' compassionate embrace of life in all its mystery and messiness. In 'A More Generous Grammar,' Davis tells us to identify her not with her pronouns but her adjectives — deep / radical / wild — and her verbs — unbind / bridge / heal. If these words describe the poet, they also describe the poems, rich with insights and imaginings that never shy from the harder truths of being alive. 'How do you encourage someone to fall / in love with the world?' Davis asks in 'Future Epigraphs.' One surefire way: Read this book."

— Lynne Knight, author of *The Language of Forgetting*

"*Italics* is a collection of meditations uttered softly, but delivered by force. Alison Davis is a poet of the lyrical observation (a bud, a blossom, a bush, a bouquet) and wild leaps ('None of us is walking a dog'). We are lulled and shocked awake by the work in this collection."

— Laura Kasischke, Rilke Poetry Prize recipient and author of *A Suspicious River*

italics

POEMS

Alison Davis

Published by Wildhouse Poetry
an imprint of Wildhouse Publishing
Boston, Massachusetts
www.wildhousepublishing.com

Design by Cambridge Creative Group

Cover image courtesy of Rachael Staudt

First edition
ISBN 978-1-961741-30-0

Printed in the United States of America

For Andrew

Because we require a loose leash, being free,
In order to keep belonging to you.

For Iman

Look lower.
Not the star. The string.

Contents

A Blessing for Those at the Edge

Maybe you walked here.
Maybe you ran here.
Maybe you followed a trail of stones, of feathers, of flowers,
of scents, of sky.
Maybe you went afoot with the Mystery & so how you got here
is also a mystery.
But here is where you are & here
is always its own kind of blessing & here
at the edge, blessings compound.

Bless those at the edge of the river
of their heart,
full of promise.

Bless those at the edge of the morning,
singing the bright face of day
into the blue.

Bless those at the edge of what they know,
watching the old certainties crumble.

Bless those at the edge of doom,
bearing it out, as the famous bard wrote,
with or without the draw of a happy ending.

Bless those at the edge of love
of self, of other, of world,
as the way forward grows more subtle, less sound.

Bless those at the edge of language,
whose tongues & tales & names
are more pledge than guarantee.

Bless those at the edge of believing
a life can be lived at the edge.

I

ALWAYS ENOUGH

Dayenu

A bud, a blossom, a bush, a bouquet.
Dayenu. Teach me, G-d, about enough. And
can you teach me gently?

*

A baby grows into a boy, enough, and walks right
into the depth of the world, also enough.
The boy's hand rearranges the desert by moving
a single grain of sand. Enough. He adds prayer. The moon
dances above the dunes. How enough. How brilliantly enough.

*

In a house in the woods, a wise one
folds a quilt and places it on a shelf.
The winter has been weathered,
and the warmth is coming. Enough.
One enough begets another: daffodils
rise in the morning rain, dough rises
beside the fire, a song rises in the heart
of the wise one, the whisper of The One
Who Will Rise disturbs the curtains.

*

We knew too much, didn't we, and so
we waited. What to call this? An almost?
The place before tears? Just be a fool
and take the step toward freedom. Teach
me, G-d, that that is enough, always
enough.

What's My Line, Part One: A Friday Afternoon

She is pouring more coffee into an almost-full mug.
It is watered down to the point of looking like whiskey.
Maybe it is whiskey.
Maybe it is muddy runoff rescued from the puddle.
She says, *jacaranda, for instance, is beautiful*
but not serious.

They are carrying a box of chalk and a stretch of sidewalk
in their dreams. The moon is never in a hurry. Tomorrow
will bring a fresh unfastening. A new haircut. A viscous voice.
Does everything seen from a distance
seem pretty? they ask.

I am contemplating loneliness again.
Sometimes joy lights a small bonfire in my hands
and warms everything I am reaching toward.
It is easy to believe touch is superfluous.
I've shaved my head, I said, *I wear robes now*
instead of dresses.

The lambkins butt heads as they slosh through the pasture,
rolling with three seasons worth of rain. The placenta is bright
with blood and earth against the gate. With an ungloved hand,
the farmer pulls back a fistful of vetch, feeds it to the ewe.
He says, *if there are fifty thousand levels of the mystery,*
maybe I'm at forty-five.

Expectations Are Not Always Resentments Waiting to Happen

I have taught myself
to expect miracles,
and so I often
get them,
one piece of evidence being
this poem,

        and *you*,

reading it.

Love Is a School of Fire

Religion isn't the theology you profess.
It isn't the way you kneel, the direction you face,
the face you present as pious, the prayers

you repeat at the appointed hours, the wine
you won't drink. It certainly isn't the commands
given to camels crossing the uncertain desert

to conquer some distant land. Nor is it the dutiful
watering of the roots, the putting of coins in a box.
It is not even the invisible dominion of Solomon's throne.

It is what you desire.

Some fall down before the golden calf. I fall down
to lick the damp earth. Clay and loam and dust
breathe me. I am not quoting any of the familiar sources.

I burn with want for whatever is. More kindling: the memories,
the music, the sermons, the girl walking weaponless in the blaze.
These words are an alternate existence. Love is a school of fire.

Poetry Belongs in Everybody's Mouth

Poetry goes well with a handful of dates at sundown,
with persimmon salad and mixed brassica slaw, dosa and idli.
It goes well with the improvised traditions of family,
like a homemade pizza on Christmas Eve,
or the established ones, like too many helpings
of Ambrosia salad and extra maraschino cherries,
with a Friday fish fry at the bingo hall.

Poetry sizzles in the pan with kimchi fried rice,
a double-portion, enough to share with the student who
has been promising to bring me some of his mother's.
Poetry simmers in the leftover corn chowder, is sprinkled
over the last slice of quiche, the one whose recipe I found
in the cancer recovery cookbook two summers ago.
Poetry sits with the runny yolk of a fried egg on rye.
Poetry in the rosemary fennel roast chicken and the
Post-Punk Kitchen vegan seitan.

Poetry slides down the throat with cinnamon tea, with cardamom
tea, with black tea sweetened with cardamom sugar,
with tea being reheated for the third time, with tea so hot
it makes the children cry. Poetry is a cup of coffee
whose grounds are waiting to be read, to tell you your future.
Poetry in homemade lemonade, homemade kombucha, a jar of beer.

Poetry brings out the bitter flavor of a fistful of miner's lettuce or
the warmth of a bowl of porridge or the freshness of backyard tomato,
juices dripping down the chin. It goes well with a slice of sourdough
and a generous pat of butter. It goes well with what my children are learning
to make on their own: pancakes, cucumber sushi, fried tofu.

Poetry likes to be paired with an aioli flight at the fancy burger place.
It wants to be doused in sriracha at the street vendor's cart. And tzatziki,

pico de gallo, salsa fresca, tapenade, honey mustard, pesto from a mason jar.
Poetry by the spoonful, poetry poured out, poetry the secret sauce.

Poetry goes well with the meals of my childhood. Borscht and duck blood soup,
kielbasa and city chicken skewers. Ask Wisława Szymborska and Czesław Miłosz.
They know. Poetry is glistening, like Anna Swir's pearls, in the cubed potatoes
in a pot of dill pickle soup. Poetry is there in the heavy pans
frying *chruściki* and *pączki* and Smucker's jam-filled *naleśniki,*
before coating them all in powdered sugar. Poetry and *pierogi*. Poetry and sauerkraut.
Poetry and cubed ham, head cheese, burnt toast. Jello molds with marshmallows inside.
Poetry and the cabbage rolls that filled the basement of the brick bungalow with
the heavy scent of onions, always stinging our eyes, always sticking to our clothes,
always following us wherever we went.

Queer Lexicon

flute: proof that holes make music possible
bolt: the hidden fingerplay of G-d behind her Maimonides light switch analogy
clue: the feather I watched fall from a crow, and when it landed at my feet, I couldn't pick it up right away.
story: the form in which any lasting truth presents itself; the form in which very persistent lies present themselves
wilt: to un-river
gale: another kind of breath

When I say *feast* I mean *my flesh*
When I say they *exhaled* I mean *we began*
When I say *angel* I mean *California condor*
When I say *faith in love* I mean *my body woven with yours*

After the Death of Her Cat, the Poet Tries to Imagine Her Ailing Father Taking One More Trip

I.

to wherever i am, national parks, our old neighborhood, probably france again—he really likes pastries, he really enjoyed carrying that baguette back to françoise's house. maybe san diego's balboa park or sunset cliffs. he used to be so thirsty for adventure that he became a truck driver. he sent me messages while i was out becoming a bible in israel and egypt. but he gave up. he abandoned his rig and took a train back from omaha because he missed home. i should have come back sooner. i shouldn't have been so gone. maybe there's still time for moscow or tokyo because it's almost unthinkable now and who said it has to be possible, who said the imagination is irrelevant.

II.

he would need his medication, which is with him everywhere these days, plus the metamucil, maybe some vitamins. does he believe in those? what does he believe in? the first time he had cancer, he asked if it would be hypocritical to start praying. mom says he wears the same thing most days, like grandpa did before he died, so the suitcase would be light. he might take *hope for today* or some other serenity-promoting reading material, but i think mom is the household librarian and the guardian of last-resort devotionals.

III.

what would he do on a trip he might never get the chance, have the courage, to take? get a bite to eat, find excuses to buy a dozen donuts. if we were together, if i asked enough, he might go for a walk with me down to the river. he'd find a coffee shop and we'd go and sit. that's probably what he'd do anywhere, in the big city or at the campground where mom made a reservation she refuses to cancel. eat something sweet, withstand an hour of adventure, like at owl canyon and red rocks, and then sleep. when it was time to leave, he would cry, visibly. a new softness, acquired at great cost.

IV.
he still wants to show me all the places he used to love. tell me their stories, like when we went on our last run together two summers back. his best friend's house. the alley where he smoked too much and sang kick out the jams by mc5. the church where he was taught to dress nice, be polite, explain god. the diamond where he played pick-up games with guys from work, the site of the factory before it was razed. he would want to show me what he remembers, that he remembers, that he has lived and that he assumed it meant something, even if now he's not so sure.

V.
would he bring anything back from these trips? maybe snacks he didn't get around to finishing. maybe a few pictures on his phone. one of my brother's kids turned on a filter, which makes all the photos look vaguely neon and blurred. we went to the art institute of chicago once, and he lingered at a warhol. i'd glorify his pictures like pop art. when i was seven or eight years old, he bought me a souvenir hat at a gas station that said "Daddy's Girl" on it. panels of neon yellow, pink, and orange. i was so happy i cried. i think his days of bright accumulation are over. i think he has embarked, gray and groping, upon the Long Letting Go.

Chain of Non-Events

Eclectic enterprise, this daily exercise of meaning-making. Ilia Delio says *wholemaking*. Wholemeal yellow corn muffins. Yellow shopping bags, reminiscent of rain slickers. Succulent stems snapped off by the rain, salvaged as cuttings, a delicate bouquet, ready to be propagated. Delicate indiscretion of a lunch discussion. Let me be indiscrete: *to a tender sapling / most of all / do I compare you.* I scrutinize, so as not to say pathologize, my posture, which could be read as tender or as bowed. Head bowed over a book, to read is to hear in silence. The music begins in silence: the capo, the tuner, the strap, all taking their places in the red spectacle. Leaf blower strapped to the man's back, its buzz, like speaker feedback, painful enough to make me wince but not enough to leave this spot. Distracted tidying reveals a sticky spot on my desk, honey most likely. *Honey-colored love light,* Alanta once wrote. Come see me in the good light, the refrain of these fresh days.

"City Square I" by Alberto Giacometti

Our bodies are long because we have walked a long
road to be here. Our doing shapes us in mysterious
ways. Skin like a sweep of leaves whipped up
on a breeze, but stronger than steel. We cast rippled shadows

when the light wanes. Can we aim for something other than
making sense? None of us is walking a dog. One among us, a woman,
or perhaps a man, or perhaps a person who only wants to be
a person, is telling a stranger the possibly true story of their birth.

Our sculptor didn't have the right tools
to include the others, the mighty invisible ones who have crossed
over, who are operating 24-hour spiritual crisis hotlines
that no one ever calls but could.

The square is sparse. Not a patch of grass or cobblestone
in sight. We make meager attempts to ungrief our faces
and recommence our commerce with the living. We all have secrets
 we are longing
to never have to tell, and that's why we never touch. But my secret is that

I am trying to touch. I am trying to become a magician so powerful
 I can make
everyone I touch, no matter how reluctant, believe they are beautiful.
A combination of declaratives and hands that can't be bested.
 Is your secret
that you dream of becoming a jasmine peddler who never runs out
 of garlands,

who weaves flowers through a city that has forgotten how to listen
to the silence of its own heart? The scent of the sea can't be far
behind. The waves are a wordless truth that settles what besieges.
What else is there to say to each other?

The Students Teach Me What to Write

Write about the ones who came to office hours every week that first year, the ones who kept coming every week, even after you weren't their teacher anymore, yes, Katie, who shared a booth and soda bread or a baked potato with you in O'Shag, who invited you home to Rochester Hills to meet her family, who traveled with you to Besançon to see the places that were still so alive in your memory, about how she was the first person who painted something that made you cry, about the breast pump and poem and Madeleine books she sent you in the mail a full decade after the last time you saw her.

Write about standing on the church steps in front of the bus stop after school on a winter morning, the lake effect sweeping icicles into your hair, where you watched Cialis and Jonathan and Carlos, where you watched Christina, Joy, Jessica, José all huddle, from the place you were paid to stand so that if a fight broke out you could do something save someone call for help although what could your stature hands head heart have done?

Write about the tactile learners, the ones who wrote poems about snow in the classroom with the faulty heater, posters of Martinique and Guadeloupe on the wall, whose floors you swept and whose boards you washed, this place you wanted students to want to be, that was supposed to be safer than the public schools with the color wars and unionized content deliverers with the Chicago winter streaming through the broken windows, we all found it hard to want things, to want what we could have.

Write about Ceni, who asked you to close the door and told you her story that was also your story, a story about bodies that don't want to be bodies anymore, a story about waking up the next day and walking around or not in a hollowed-out version of yourself all raw marrow all exposed all clinging to life anyway.

Write about Nikki reading a Bible verse at your wedding and Kelsey signing up for your section of French after meeting you at the gym and Deepak who gave you bottles of wine for your birthday and

Jenny who bought every single item on your baby registry when your first was born. Write about Michael whose mother said either pre-med or no money and why throw away your time at Stanford on what you could get on a trip abroad and a few days at the local library. Write write write about Michel who took you to the ballet with his sister, Colleen with her cornrows who left after three classes to join the Peace Corps but not before you gave her a postcard that read *On peut toujours replanter un arbre; un homme c'est plus difficile*. Write about Erica who loved being Cuban and Flight of the Conchords.

Write about the thank you cards in both directions. Write about the comments on their essays. Write about writing "this is important" and "this made me cry" and "you are holding back." Write about the suicide notes and excuses and lies and dedications and requests for extensions. Write about the ones who couldn't write but could talk, talk all day, tell you something real when looking into your eyes, when looking at a picture of your kid holding your cat, when looking out past the amaranth towering in the garden.

Write about Nammy. Never stop writing about Nammy.

Write about spending a week in the wilderness, among the foxglove and yarrow, a week in the mist of the tumultuous coast, between the estuary and the sea, where you noticed Patrick and Nico deciding that fear wasn't a thing, that their life was the only thing and that it was only a life if they were towering above the others, above the gulls, with their hearts beating preposterously in their chests. Write about Chloe below, the first one to brave the waves and about Iman who noticed. Write about everything that Iman noticed, notices, with her life helps you to notice. Write about the burning sensation of that gift in your eyes, the unbearable beauty it coaxes you into seeing. Write about how they carried you when you fainted. Write about how they are still carrying you.

Write about the ones who died, Parker and Nico. Daniel. Write about the ones who left, Oliver and Isabelle and Chloe and Charlotte. Sohm left before you even got to know him. Tara left and is dancing in her own shadow. Zia left and wears bras as shirts and still says hi to you in the park when you cross paths.

Write about Mona, who was all double-jointed and awkward, who could barely carry her books but wanted to be the base of the pyramid and who were you to turn her away. Write about how her father was late to pick her up every week after practice, so you sat on the steps of the gymnasium while the AA meeting took place behind you, waiting for his tired taxi to pull up. Mohammed always said *salaam aleikoum*, though he never knew your name.

Write about Laurent, who didn't want to be a refugee but was, who cried when you confronted him about letting another student copy his homework, who came to your apartment on the last day of school to get all your Firefly DVDs and said thank you for giving me back my imagination.

Write about Jocelyn, who thought she was fat, but then discovered she was strong. Write about Allen who brought you preserved lemons and just wanted to talk. Write about Enzo roaming the streets of Santa Rosa with packets of cigarettes in his pockets, hoping to use them to befriend homeless people and find out what they need, who wants to give them what they need, who calls the cops on the underage drinkers and still plays Magic. Write about praying with Lukas, meditating with Erin, singing with Alanta, dancing with Savannah. Write about what their parents tell you and what they are trying to hide.

Write about taking your own kids to the park and thinking of them, always thinking of them. Write about sending Tony off to bed while you stay up reading journal entries. Write about Finn waving to you at the stoplight. Write about Jordan waving to you from his driveway. Write about Geneva buying all of your groceries when you bump into her at the store.

Write about the ones who take your picture without you knowing and send it to you later with a thank you and a smile. Write about how you can't stop writing about what they write, how they write, why they write. Write because it's nonsense, nonsense to walk through this life with so many others' feet in your heart, but here you are still trodding and is this the miracle that you haven't known how to ask for?

Pass It On

The rhetoric of alarm, of obligation, leaves much to be desired.
Give me the rhetoric of awe.

The clairvoyance of our ancestors is an unnamed bone
in our body. The shoes we wear may be marvelously sewn,

but the soul has no need of such luxuries. Still,
feet are not extraneous. Every thing without a body

longs for one. Ask: how many types of cereal can you name
the mascot for? Can you extrapolate that knowledge

to other domains? Kings of France? State flowers?
Elements on the periodic table? Ask: when the time is right,

is there any force that can stop it?

The primary task of this lifetime is to learn
your own alphabet, the one you were born with.

Imagination is a bridge you must cross to find it.
As long as you remain on the shore, nothing can be

unintentionally beautiful, which is to say, life cannot grow
beyond calculations, stays far too small. Itches get scratched,

classes get dismissed, and the same old songs
make you cry for the same old reasons. On the other side,

one poppy, among other poppies, root-risen and sugar-bright,
moving. You will be able to watch it write itself

a new name, a true name, maybe even yours.

The Museum of Inquiry

How much of what we see is a product of our eyes?
Light and shadow are trying to have a conversation inside a box,
    a case, a frame.
Yes, and could it be otherwise?

If dots walk far enough across the canvas, we call them lines.
If we caught them waltzing on the ceiling, would they need a
    new name?
How much of what we see is a product of our eyes?

O'Keefe needed abstraction. Chagall lived on nothing but skies.
In my own heart, it is admittedly much the same.
Yes, and could it be otherwise?

It may take more than one lifetime to realize
That most of what we put on display perpetuates a petty game.
How much of what we see is a product of our eyes?

Inquiry is as artful as a sculpture. Can questions vessel like clay dries?
In the absence of a quick answer, even the artist rushes to blame.
Yes, and could it be otherwise?

What of the curator's bewilderment and the seeker's private surprise?
From the gap between two deep truths, the heart looks out, takes aim.
How much of what we see is a product of our eyes?
Yes, and could it be otherwise?

A Poem the Fact Checker Would Likely Approve of

Some threats of war remain threats,
and others become battles, remind us that evil is not an abstraction.

The ticker ticks along the bottom of the screen,
and the calculations beget more calculations.

The wild grapes grow in sturdy tangles.
Pumpkins sprout from the compost heap.

You can winnow out in the field
or in front of the flame.

Joy is no less a grenade than grief,
can wipe out the established shape of a life in moments.

At the moment of death, beyond the reach of telescopes,
whatever he saw he *loved*.

I am trying to say something about the grandness of our knowing
and its factual limits.

The Poets Make Uncertaintea on a Saturday Afternoon

The teapot is a pocket that collects light, not lint.

Instead of going to the acupuncturist, I slow-dance with the cacti. It's not without love.

Sage tea, the color of gas station coffee, dribbles down the spout and puddles on the tablecloth. It should stain the white cotton. How does it disappear so quickly?

The right wing is on a caffeine crash. Today I am the left wing, and I don't drink caffeine because it turns my bones inside out. I bought some Ghazal instant coffee for the morning. I didn't intend for that to be poetic. Rumi is going on about the wine again. A new kind of drunkenness, daring us out of that old world.

We pour the past into small cups. It tastes familiar, but I can't put my finger on it. A hint of growth, of blackberry, of those brambles beside the road. Handfuls of fresh fruit, staining our fingers,wild with possibility.

My acupuncturist says that I fidget too much while I'm on the table.

The last time I went to Ojai, I stayed in a yurt with an outdoor shower. Next time, I'll be staying in a trailer with no shower at all. I'm assuming the morning will make me fresh, awake, even a kind of clean.

If that doesn't work, *tough titties*. There's no back-up plan. It's morning mist or bust.

The tea leaves at the bottom of the pot are huddled to one side. That means there's safety in numbers. That means there's safety. That means I can sip myself safe.

The glass beads of uncertainty are scattered across the floor. Watch your step.

The red flasks of remembering are stacked on the highest shelf. You'll need a sturdy ladder to reach them.

You can never reach them.

When the fortune-teller takes a sip of sage tea, she starts to float, and her teeth rearrange themselves in her mouth. She's not sure if that makes things easier or harder to swallow.

Ali Cat is falling out of toe stand again. Should have stayed in tree pose. She has a lot to learn about roots.

If you plan on making that tea cake, you will need to go to the store. You're out of baking powder. And patience.

The potter threw the mug on a broken wheel. The potter fired the vase in a glacial kiln. The potter closed up shop on a lucky Sunday.

When it stops raining, the lemonade will be ready. We're sick of drinking tea. We're sick of intoning *Allah, with this warmth, dissolve anything that is blocking my heart*. What can I do with this stone inside of me?

The teapot is holding a press conference but will not be taking questions. *Merci à tous d'être venus.*

The glass beads are rolling back into the bag, and I cinch it shut.

The World of Things (Wants Me)

Laces, skates, children's hands.
We weave shapes around the rink, wide and wild.
We sing along when we know the words.
I know all the words, so I am always singing.

Rain jackets, boots, bags, children's hands.
We form a chain and walk out into the morning.
The storms have turned the street into a mirror.
Earth is just a reflection of sky.

Cups, plates, nachos, children's hands.
We are not ashamed of our hunger, our bodies.
We eat until we feel fed, wash the dishes, practice spelling.
e-u-c-a-l-y-p-t-u-s.

Pillow, blanket, cushion, my own hands.
Each night, I ask a pilgrim to deliver me to the world of sleep.
Usually one of them says yes, and
together we make *poustinia* in the dark.

II

THE FIRE FROM THE DRAGON

If the Point Were to Tell It Straight, not Slant

In our first session, I told my tutor how much I used to love to take my siblings to the park when they were little. He said *Oh, so you had to help raise them?* No, not really, *it was just for fun*. Climbing trees and picking apricots and playing fetch with the dalmatians that were always there on Saturday mornings. He said, *So you needed to get out of the house to have fun? Tell me more about that.* He asked questions that didn't fit my life so I could write a story that didn't fit my life but did fit the genre. *Everyone embellishes,* he said. The struggle is what makes the hero. *Then maybe I should write about my parent's divorce?* A frown. *Oh, God, no. That's been done to death.*

*

I wasn't the star of the play, but I was in it. I wasn't the star of the team, but I was on it. I wasn't the president of the club, but I went to all the meetings. I didn't win the competition, but I tried. I'm good at public speaking and applying liquid eyeliner. I rotate my date night underwear, but I'm not sure if I've ever been in love. My parents still brag that I potty-trained myself, that I was the first person in my class to learn to read. My favorite thing about school is when it's over. In the hollow of a tree at the far end of the parking lot, I keep a collection of things that have been lost or left behind: a Post-it note with a 209 phone number, a brass key, a conch shell charm, a souvenir penny from Yosemite, a lipstick, the wing of a swallowtail butterfly, the promises of my childhood.

*

Things that are more important right now: planning my spring break trip, sponsoring a voter registration drive, working at In-N-Out, pretending to be vegan to impress a girl, sleeping in, sleeping around, photographing treetops, playing D&D, disappearing, losing twenty pounds, gaining twenty pounds, vaping in the bathroom, hiding my eating disorder, solo kayaking the Green River, memorizing the capitals of every country in the world, learning to surf, sneaking out after curfew, raising money for Syrian refugees, walking the dog, dyeing my sister's hair blue, breaking the cycle of intergenerational trauma, planting succulents and ponytail palms, writing a screenplay, lying about why this is the best I could do, re-learning how to dream.

*

They keep telling me to find my passion. My voice. My story. But none of the adults in my life have even done that, so how am I, at seventeen, supposed to? I keep having a dream where I'm ice skating on a pond, and a dragon appears, sets a ring of pines ablaze. The flames melt the ice, and I fall in. I flail in the water. The fire closes in on me. Unable to save myself, I let my legs go limp and say goodbye. But my skates bump up against something in the water. I realize I can touch, that I could have been touching the whole time, and walk right out. On the shore, the fire from the dragon keeps me from freezing, and I watch the stars spell out my most intimate questions in the sky. I lay there for a long time, listening—

Arriving Is Rarely the Point of the Story

—after the photograph "Lighthouse at the Edge of the World"
by G.G. Silverman

I.

This is not the cover of a Virgina Woolf novel, and it does not have an ending. It is not a zoo where animals are rehabilitated or a Russian tea room. It is not a place that exists only in my imagination. It's not a picture of my bones or my breath. It's not a picture of a mistake. It's not a mistake.

II.

Whose birthday is it? Are the travelers safe?
Can concrete be trusted? Who else is still searching for the light?
Is it going to rain? Why do we see so dimly?
How cold is the water, and what is my responsibility toward it?

How did gray become a *miracle*?

III.

Lighthouses are good at reminding us that deep sighs are just shy of deep breaths, which we need.

Lighthouses are not good at migration or wearing cotillion gowns.

Lighthouses are really good at posing for pictures.

Lighthouses are rarely good at cleaning out the attic, judiciously deciding what to keep.

IV.

Two women holding hands, walking to the edge of the earth. A trail of lupines beating the odds. The asphalt, built to withstand pounding, full of potholes and cracks where large ghosts have passed too heavily, too often. A street sign with an outdated name. The hands of the photographer, lovingly adjusting the lens. The heart of the photographer, which is, in fact, is the lens itself.

V.
We could call her:

After the Long Winter
Grandma Wilma's Lonely Body
Old Intentions
A Close-Up of the Panorama
Arriving Is Usually Part of the Story
Arriving Is Rarely the Point of the Story
Why Everything Is Trying to Become a Stronghold of the Spirit

VI.
To capture what is left of the light is a labor of love.
We crawl into and out of mysterious spaces
where navigation loses its appeal and lostness
yields to here, to *right here*, to this celebration
of sea and seeing, of sky and shore. The coast
is an invitation for opposites to touch,
to keep touching and never let go.

Future Epigraphs

—for Andrew Sullivan

I'm always sitting in the front row,
and I'm almost always scribbling. Or, lately, painting,
if my characterization of time is generous because
late have I much learned. I roughly sketch a man I love,
slender and soulful, wearing an infinity scarf,
and give him a speech bubble that says:

When you're more concerned with how it looks
than what it is, you're performing.

I am concerned with how it looks, and concerned
about what my concern says about me, and by *it,*
I mean my sketch, my self, the algorithms, the curve
of the f that could have been slightly more elegant if
I hadn't been scurrying to get out in block letters
the next stepping stone on the path of honest thought:

A liar still has a relationship to truth,
but a bullshitter doesn't.

He says the children are coming to light candles
that have never been lit. He says the teachers
are learning to give hope a home where hope
has never resided. I am not saying, but I am
thinking, my body will be an altar where
consecration is no longer an abstraction.

People do not want to be told what to know.
They want to be seen.

But seen by whom? And seen with what eyes?
Between the banal and the horrific, many are trying
to make a buck. They trade in the music

for the metronome, except that the music is children, is
people, is life, and the metronome eventually flatlines
every thing into any thing into no real thing.

In jazz, the rules are not the end game.
They are in service of free play.

Now I am doodling again, carnations, maybe,
because marigolds have too many memories,
and I am threading them with my pen,
with thin black lines, without knowing what direction
they will go in next. They refuse the predictable limits
of my imagination. In tiny letters, I print,

Stringing together old thoughts might make
a beautiful garland, but it cannot make a garden.

It's unclear if knowing is always a power play. It's unclear
the extent to which we can ensoul things when
efficient causation is imposed upon us all the way down,
no matter how much vaguely poetic rhetoric we dress it up in.
It's unclear if we, if I, will be a beautiful exception. The man
I love pauses. He folds his hands at his chin, in reverence:

How do you encourage someone to fall
in love with the world?

Field Notes from the Chinstrap Penguins: 3,960 Tries to Get It Done

83. The mate is too close, the wind too strong. The mate is too far, the night too long. Six seconds of respite, then back at it.

102. Twinkle, twinkle, little heart, how I wonder where you aren't.

248. Housing insecurity steadies the stare. They want to study us in our natural habitat, but how much longer will we have one? Those who lord over the land are subtly evicting us. Eyes closed to drop into what's real: rest, the breadth three deep breaths.

816. Whalesong lullaby. Quick shut-eye.

1,325. Gossip, whipped up, sails in on the surface of the waves. *He never came back from the hunt. She's looking a little gaunt. Who's sleeping with whom?* Shit, they heard us. Close your eyes! Pretend to be asleep! Nothing but windtalkers here.

1,582. Oil-slick feathers, crowning the face of a beloved. Drift off a moment. Short and sweet, such dreams.

1,969. Neighbors stop by for a visit. Kelp gulls quell the group with their stories of the incomprehensible blue. What do you, on the edge of the otherworld, dare to believe?

2,570. We're not nocturnal. We're not diurnal. Does that mean we transcend time? Twelve seconds to consider.

2,941. Quick, the baby's down already. Don't waste this chance. A shared snooze.

3,202. The bedtime prayer is as natural as breath. Always: bless and release.

3,960. The totals are in. Eleven hours in the universal astral. Don't bother doubting the existence of our souls—or yours, for that matter. We've consolidated the messages we're always returning with: nothing, not a single second, wasted.

Notes to Self

—after Aracelis Girmay

you who are willing to crouch down, lean on haunches, strain for the
sake of staying low,
who look for ants and centipedes, calloused heels, discarded bits of
paper, and the promise of a word or two that can still be of some use,
you who will indeed use and create with what others have thrown
away,
you
are who i love

you who jotted down on a whim: *some words stick like glue / require a tremendous and terrible effort to remove / Some words stick like glue / are in fact the only thing keeping me together,*
you
are who i love

you ministering to the almost-alive, attracting the hummingbirds, putting away the pots with missing lids, begrudgingly granting yourself a seventy-seventh second chance, adding a little more salt to the broth, writing letters that make you cry. you willing to write this poem before it was one, wild with what was and what isn't yet and whom it will cost to live this way,
you and you
and you are who

What's My Line, Part Two: Fever Is How the Body Prays

Her fever has finally broken.
The doctor told her to surrender to the sickness,
to let the spiritual world do its work.
Everything that needs to leave the body eventually will.
That was the doctor's polite way of saying
STOP BEING ON THE SHIT YOU'RE ON.

In one of the fever dreams, the girl came back again.
Her voice was twelve thousand turkey tail mushrooms
growing on the side of a wattle house. She didn't mention the promises
or the parachutes. She held her own body like a green feather and said
if you're not going to touch the world with all your being,
do you even deserve arms

The others kept their appointments while she was on fire.
The lawyer might have been wearing a suit, but his voice
on the line was naked and ashamed of itself. They've decided
to close down all the bathrooms in that building. The parade
isn't being postponed. The magpies are still forming circles in the rain.
A note on the calendar reads *who taught you that the weaving is the work?*

Souvenirs

a white skirt a black backpack
a basket of figs
a pair of bus tickets
he never told me where
we were going
& i didn't care. *yalla,* let's go,
the going together
was enough.

on the ride, my head
on his shoulder
old men cupping their hands
at the appointed hour
praying perhaps that
this day
would take us
somewhere we want to be
inshallah &
that prayer is alive still—

when the post card arrives
after a long silence
the envelope bears my maiden
name. a decade
since the beach
disappearing at high tide,
singing love songs
to the wild goats on the bluff,
their left legs longer
than their right from lifetimes
of scaling mountains
of walking the edge
of the world.
we all adapt
to our surroundings

in order to stay.
i didn't take a single photograph.

along the american river trail
i use my fingers to trace
ripples in the sand. i am willing
to be startled into
remembering:
a row of white stucco
houses crashing
against the blue sea
the blue sky
the bruised-blue belief
that there's something whole
on the other side
of all this
                                        unknowing.

the sidewalk runs out
he took my hand
he's reaching out
i am meeting
him somewhere new
somewhere green
calling out   *ya habibi—*

Abbondanza

—for Daniel D'Agostini

He is a good farmer and a fervent lover of god-
forsaken people. They come to him
because something in them knows *this dirt*
is where we came from. Some are braiding
at the edge of the field because their hearts
have to be remade before their hands
can be of more use. When the time comes, he blows out
the candle and latches the door.
A coyote howls, its breath turning
the air to gold. The farmer can see it shimmer,
a dance in the dazzling dark. Each seed
goes to work under the rays of the moon,
as round and as full as the dream of a lover's belly.
Growth is chthonic.
The incantations crack the sky—
open.

Cundrie

We turn over stones along the path, looking for words
that might be hiding underneath their slick skin. You never

know who will whisper wild language, damp & cool
to the touch. Brash as the crow's call. *Saint Crow.*

Cundrie spit truth like gravel beneath a tire & her tusks
dripped with grease & godspeak. The retinue gasped, exposed.

On the ridge we commemorate this humiliating & necessary
exposure, one by one through basalt & serpentinite & gabbro.

Lifting, tossing, turning, stacking.   Pausing.   Many are holding
the oracles up to their ears in an expectation that, if feigned,

feels convincing. Why do we spend so many of our days
worshiping the thin dust along the surface of what can be said?

We stoop & turn & stand, stoop again. Pill bugs scatter. A tangle
of thin, gray roots strangled by silt. One boy palms a stone,

oval-shaped & egg-white, hurls it at the cragged face
of the embankment, eager to see what secrets might break free.

Bus Tour of the Emeryville Superbloom

The woman standing at the front of the bus
says only one thing to the driver: *it's always about the energy,*
the energy, the energy. I can't tell how she means it, if

she means it. Her visor is pulled down low
over her eyes, and her hands, tattooed with gothic
script, fish out cellophane-wrapped hard candies

from a shopping bag. She walks down the aisle, handing out
what is only hers for a moment. Most of the passengers
say no with a shake of the head. I say *thank you*, extending my hand,

and she smiles. Who am I to refuse a small kindness?
Like when the man on the Amtrak last spring
reached over to me with a bag of peanut M&Ms and a story.

We spent two hours stranded on the tracks outside Jack London Square,
where some desperate people had pushed an abandoned car
onto the tracks. They waited to watch the train collide

with the rusted skeleton and then ran away. The conductor
told us it happens all the time. The intersection of people getting
somewhere and people with nowhere to go. From inside

that air-conditioned train, patience was a relatively easy option.
Now, the woman takes a seat in front me, starts to hum
mysteriously and rocks herself back and forth, body

swinging as if between epochs. I wonder where
she's headed. I wonder why she's headed there. The man next to me
scrolls through pictures of the coastal superbloom hundreds of miles

away, oranges and pinks so absurdly alive they can be seen
from space. Visitors flock, like starlings, to the oceanside plains.
Isn't adventure always somewhere else? In front of us, the city rises

up like a sawtooth wave. Rash and insistent. The bus holds us tightly,
pulls up to a red light. A small median overflows with poppies
and lupines,
with cornflowers, mustard, and chinese houses, planted only by a
wise wind,

tended only by the heart's unyielding need for riots
of color. I look into their faces, and they look back. At green, the
bus belches,
moves forward. They wave us on. Wild, even here, is a vital ancestry.

The Moth

The mail carrier asked me.
The elderly power-walker wearing stirrup pants asked me.
The man with the pomegranate tree on Laura Lane asked me.
The woman driving the black sedan didn't ask me, but she idled
at the four-way stop for over a minute. I counted.
The sun might have asked me, but the wind got in the way.

Are you okay?

I was crouching at the corner
where a wounded moth
was trying to scamper
out of the gutter
and fly away.
I watched its legs.
I watched each straining wing,
flecked with orange and chestnut.
The left one looked lame.
I asked to get closer.
On the asphalt, I could see
what looked like blood
on its thorax. I asked,

Are you okay, blessed one?

The mail carrier drove away.
The power-walker turned the corner.
The man went inside.
The black sedan disappeared behind the oaks.
The sun was patient.
The moth and I spoke,
words that must be kept secret,
and we parted ways.

On the walk back
to where I came from,
I took a handful of dandelion seeds
and fingered them into my hair.

My body is a place
where wild things can grow.

The Beauty Playlist

My daughter makes up her own songs
about swimming in the river and loving me

more than bridges, beaches, and salmon bones.
She is five, and the world appears to her

mostly good, although we both teared up at the sight
of a dead squirrel at the end of the driveway,

although the news of this war and that war and
all the other wars shift the sands we stand on.

What she knows is that we boxed up her old cloth diapers
and sent them to Ukraine. What she sees is her older sister

selling lemonade and donating the money to the children
in Gaza who deserve sweetness, not desperate thirst.

What she hears is a gut-cry and the silk of a gospel song.
Every night, we pray: *make me an instrument of thy peace.*

In the morning, the light touches their small bodies
with its delicate hands. We sing: *yonder come day*

and walk out into a burst of plum blossoms in the breeze,
the only snow they know. On a hike, we collect feathers

and bleached twigs to build an altar by our favorite blue oak.
The river dances in the distance. We hold hands all the way home.

Prairie Haibun: Between Two Storms

We gather juniper berries and dandelion greens along the trail. We ask before we pick, and we sing thanks while our hands and hearts move over stems and branches. We are all bodies, full of wild. I don't come from the People of the Walaheen. I don't come from the People of the Buck Moon. I come from beech rosary beads and ninety-five grievances. I come from in search of a new world life. But I am of the earth, a native species. I am trying to live non-invasive. Last month's storms, next month's storms, every season's storms, will wash away something cherished, and what will we do with that space? The water is murky, but our vision, at least for a moment, is clear: space is another word for *spirit*. When our baskets are full, we walk over to the creek and play where crawfish zig zag their way from one slick rock to the next. The child beside me and the child inside me greet them as friends. We ask them what they need. A life where the balance between giving and receiving is rarely tipped is a language I haven't learned yet. I stumble through the perceived silence, through the inflections of the fawns in the meadow and the emphases of the black swallowtails among the milkweed. Back at home, we char the juniper and roast corn in its ash. We give thanks for its flesh, now flecked inky blue, indigo

as deep as night sky
where sleep will return
us to our knowing.

For Now

She swings her hammer against the blue.
Easy was never really an option.
Color flies forth from her strike.
Her body is well-trained to shoulder other people's sins.
For all we know, when we get to the horizon,
we are going to drop off the edge of the world.

My biography is an exercise in the occult significance of forgiveness.
I am singing a very old song, one that I haven't finished learning.
The lyrics are written on stones on the far edge of the other island.
Who will teach me to swim?
You have to stop thinking you're in the wrong place.

Time's Other Green Orchards

Today is when the lightning and thunder come at four p.m. and blow
spring back a few weeks. It is when the strawberries take their
first flecks
of red from the earth, and when the girl's mother, in tears, asks if we
can pray. Her soul's only remaining strategy is a Hail Mary,

and she's still throwing the ball, even though all the other players
have left the field, and all the fans are filing out of the stadium.

She holds my hands and looks up at the scrub oak,
blinking back disbelief.
Today is a promise longer than my body,

longer than anybody, enough for every body.

Yesterday was when we decided to be born, to come inching
into a world that has a lot to offer, if you don't mind the mess

of becoming. I was willing to leave the world
of the spirit. Last night at sunset, the shopkeepers pulled

down their gates, passed out dates, and stood talking in the alley
a while. They swapped almost-true stories of past pilgrimages

and made more plans because time is a mysterious neighbor
who is always knocking on your door, asking you to
borrow something

you're pretty sure you just ran out of yesterday.

Tomorrow isn't when the healing will be finished. Tomorrow doesn't know
its true name, but it answers to as many as there are voices
calling out

to it. *The next right thing. Daughter of now. Trip number four*
hundred sixty-seven to the buffet of regret. It's later than you think,

but it's not over. Will the mother's tears have dried, or will they still
be feeding the river of grief that flows northwest from the spleen,
toward the trees,

toward the stars? The men will open the shop, make coffee, face
east to pray.
Their tongues are alive, like mine. What will be on our hearts?

Tomorrow's certainty applies only to its unfolding.

Shadow Work

The Great Below
is full of soothsayers.
They have a thousand
dark & holy faces—
worm & loam,
rodent & bone.
Let them out.
Let them all out.
Then listen
to what they have
to say.

Human hearts must
learn how to
detect the difference
between mere prediction
and prophecy. We need
the wisdom those lowly ones
have gathered in the womb
of the world.

Hoping for spring
is too obvious. The long
winter, the bare birches—
take me to those mysteries.
The doe's den is covered
in frost, and she never
shivers. Bring me beyond
the predictable preference
for warmth.

Once we embrace
it, isn't the shadow side
its own kind of blessing

because it points back
toward something *real*?

All seeing requires a mixture
of darkness & light.
It's a matter of
adjusting the eyes
of the soul.

Today, I decide to walk into a future
from which everyone else
is running.

The Yellow Gate

I can't really understand why I didn't give up, given all the figures that I had in front of me to say that it wasn't going to be possible.
—Jasmin Paris

It gets in your bones,
this kind of desire,
this kind of fire.

The fire speaks
into and out of the mountains,
the burrs and brambles and stones,

the white snakeroot, the swamp milkweed,
the stars that come and go as you run
for two and a half days. As you run from

a past in which you couldn't make it.
As you run toward
a future in which you finish,

even though you get lost.
Everyone gets lost, but the fire still knows
your name. Ten thousand feet

above sea level, six times over,
your feet trace a long, wordless prayer.
What is it to believe

that we can reach such heights?
With twenty-two seconds to spare,
you touch the yellow gate.

There is an intimacy with life
that only deep struggle can summon.
That is the medal you drape around your neck.

In the Hills

We sit in silence around the fire.
The light is leaving
the sky overhead,
but in front of us
the world is
a bright mountain
willing to burn.

The shape we make is sacred.
The stories that spill out of us
are sacred. There is nothing
outside the kingdom
of sacred
because we have been broken
open.

Months ago
the rain fell and
the river rose.
The dry bones
of the earth
became flesh again
and danced with the coyotes.

We know because
we were there,
watching, learning.
We know because
that is where we were taught
to build this fire.

Summer will bleach
what winter muddied
and in between we start to feel
our true colors.

Black oak crackles.
Embers collapse
under the weight
of their own heat. A song
like a storm
we refuse
to take shelter from
rises in the smoke. The stones
are never silent. They sing:

> *In this circle, no fear.*
> *In this circle, deep peace.*
> *In this circle, new confidence.*
> *In this circle, safety.*

Menstruation Haibun at Sinkyone Wilderness State Park

We are all singing a song about birds this time, and though our voices are strong, our breath fierce, it is not we who make the limbs of the redwood dance. I am still always looking for treetops, and I am still always looking for stones, which means I don't know which way to look. Cow's parsnip and columbine flank the trail, and the light pours through between the pines. Each step becomes deliberate. To inhabit my body among all the earth-bodies, this is the most ecstatic tale of flesh on flesh. Later we sit in a circle at Anderson Gulch and carve spoons with hot coals and sharp knives. Sweet smoke, strong stroke. We sweat and tell stories worth telling, whether they are true or not. Renegade summers. River-wild loves. Cliff jumping from one incarnation to the next. When I stand, I wipe the seat of my pants and come away with a smear of blood on my fingertips. *In this moment, the new initiate is claimed.* For four days, my body makes a great display, far away from the city comforts that let us hide our bodies, hide from our bodies, their secretions and smells and soft-spoken rhythmic wisdom. They all know. We are still singing when we reach Wheeler Beach, now about the sun rising in our souls, and I keep the song alive as I wash at the edge of the creek. I offer my blood with that of the fox and the doe and field mouse and birthing Mother and, yes, with everything that has been wounded or left dead on this precious earth, and I stay in the story that what I need in this moment is already here. I stay, I stay, I stay in the story that

my blood will bind me
to the solid, hallowed ground
and be my glory.

Two California Condors Stage a Takeover of the Baltimore Catechism, Volume 2, Lessons 1–7

Q: Who made us?
A: God didn't not make us & God didn't make us alone & God didn't unmake us.

Q: Who is God?
A: My deepest me. Your deepest you. The sky from which all wings are born. Certainly not *a* being. Certainly another name for *being itself*.

Q: Why did God make us?
A: We have a lot to learn about love and attention.

Q: What must we do to cultivate our love and attention?
A: Up here on the trails, the parents are always hurrying their children on. *Come on, let's go, keep it moving, just a little farther.* The children have better things to do than get somewhere. For example, being here. The dust, the serpentine, the swallowtail and painted lady, the wild mustard, the child—all together in being here on this map of time, which is what humans call a mountain, singing a song of life.

Q: From whom do we learn to love?
A: See above.

Q: Where do we find the chief truths?
A: See above and below.

Q: Recite the Apostles' Creed.
A: We believe in *viriditas*, in the greening from within, in the factual miracle of our own aliveness. We believe in the life pouring through us, which did not begin and will not end with us. We believe in the pain and the rising, in the gap and the pause, in the primal flaring forth, in the readiness to receive warmth and light. We believe in the everyday alchemy of dying and becoming, which have never

been separate phenomena. We believe in the range where we were released to start again, in starting again, and in the goodness in the researchers' hearts. We believe in what hearts know, what hearts grow, what hearts let show, and the joyful challenges ahead. *Per omnia saecula saeculorum, amen*.

Toward Regulus

At dawn, the sheep follow the shepherdess
up the ridge to graze in the manzanita grove.
The path is long, and so is the day.

While the sheep poke through trees, the shepherdess
pokes through memories, like barley straw in a picnic blanket.
Last summer, river rocks and packing tape.

The one before, loquats and the ache,
a body lost and found. Pride of Madeira pushing
through the chain link fence. Sinai, Montara Mountain,

Deauville. Some memories are lodged so deeply
in whatever her life is woven out of that she gives up
on trying to shake them free.

In late afternoon, the shepherdess follows the sheep,
who instinctively file down to the creek.
The water runs cool but not clear.

Transparency is not a universal virtue.
Everyone drinks for a while. No one loses their footing.
The day wears itself in a crown of light that wraps

around the whole ranch, the whole ridge, the whole range
of what can be felt between here and the sky,
while the nearby field, littered with yesterdays, shouts resurrection.

A clawfoot bathtub cracked from rim to limb alive again
with St. John's wort and coyote mint. The bones
of an old stable shelter a trio of fawns who hear time ripen.

Moss on a defunct septic tank seems to spell out the word
yes. Wasn't it time for a sign? At sunset, the sheep
and the shepherdess return to the barn, where the sheep remain.

Without them, the last of the light blooms large, indolent. Quiet.
Without them, the shepherdess is just a girl beneath the four royal stars,
slowly undoing her exile from the quarters of the heavens.

III

AT THE EDGE OF THE WILD

Setting Out

A gentle satisfaction with the view
from the window below, fondness for a warm bed.
The neighbor that brings daisies on a Sunday afternoon
and insists on helping to knead the dough.
The children who gather and run around the square stoop
to double knot their laces when they come untied.
Fine and good comings and goings.

Aren't most of us content with a postcard or two
from these well-rehearsed days? Isn't life in the valley
usually enough to turn a golden phrase, ensure a certain
continuity, fill a basket with barley and light?

Sometimes it is necessary to say goodbye; even
very good things often disguise the insidious bookkeeping
of who owes, who owns, who loans, who enforces the ranks,
who maintains the files in order to keep the ledgers full.

We heard some were seeking a different story, so we went
to listen. They made villages halfway up the face
of the ominous mountain. Sprawl yielding to dwellings
that are sturdy, sparse, molded out of a pact
with the sacred. Bodies, masterpieces of the earth,
shoulder each other beneath the open sky. Fires burn bright.
In summer, huckleberry, in winter, hare. The law of the seasons
prevails, a fiercely earned comfort. Songs are currency.

Couldn't we have lived a century
there at the edge of the wild? Wouldn't the winds have shaped
our souls into something vast and deep as we split wood
and gathered for the ceremony?

The caves on the other side of the threshold kept calling, calling
calling us by names we had never heard before
but knew were ours. *Darkstream. Lightgarden. Childgod.*

What's My Line, Part Three: Hafiz Wishes His Spiritual Progeny a Happy Birthday

In one version of the story, they grow old together and remember
everything. Any changes happen in tandem, at least enough of the time.
They don't fight over the channel or the bank account or
which constellation
is which. They have a favorite waitress at their favorite restaurant,
and loneliness is a secretive friend that never wants to come over.
So vast a room your soul, every universe can fit into it.

In another version of the story, they grow old together and remember
enough to know how much has been forgotten. Change grows
like mustard,
and they quibble over the teacher's teachings, what to make of a future
that is not promised. They each have a favorite form of escape: the woods,
the flickering light. Hope may have one foot out the door,
but she is not gone.
Anything you once called beautiful, anything that ever
gave you comfort waits to unite with your arms again.

While the story is under construction, time and the mind have their own
mysterious truths to sort out, especially the ones that undermine
every version
of every plot that anyone has ever tried to plod through. When we
finally break
in the heavy boots after years of blisters, our feet have lost track
of where
we were going. The map is out of date. We are squinting at the sky.
I promise.

Seven More Psalms

—for Paul Simon

I.
Give me a question
that can't be answered
except with my life.
My whole life.
Give me grief-vessels
and green vials
full of memories,
a capo and the blues
that never gave up
the game.

II.
We all have to choose
things we can't
foresee. To be fierce
with reality and to dance
with feet made of clay.
After the rain comes,
and the troubled water recedes,
we ask to be remade.
Every time.

III.
A voice that has loved
the silence enough to know
when to break it
is a kind of heaven. My G-d
has hands
at the ends
of your arms.
All that you've held
has become holy.

IV.
Darkness is still an old friend,
even older now. It never tires
of a heart willing
to feel. Songs startle us
back to the beginning
of all music. Songs remember
us before we were heaps
of dust, sounds
built out of an exquisite
wish.

V.
The journeys of his body
have been well-rehearsed.
Each organ knows its way
home, where love is waiting.
The routes
are as circuitous as ever,
but lost is no longer a necessary
part of the vocabulary.

VI.
Stones softened by the light.
An unbroken song.
Age does and undoes itself
in the same movement.
Each *amen*
inevitable.

VII.
I am still listening for a future
bigger than a moonrise over
an open field.

Almost Forty

What we are ready and willing to give up
is different from what we must die to.

I knew a woman who gave *into* candy for Lent.
She smiled easily, but for twenty years

she had been chasing someone else's ideal
body, forcefully chipping away at her form, as if some

marble masterpiece might be waiting within. She ate
handfuls of jellybeans, of Hershey's kisses, each day.

Racked up indulgences. But diet culture doesn't die
easily. The Queen of Patriarchs always dressed

in the same shapeless cloak while we clocked laps
on the dirt trail around the lakes. At home,

I clapped my running shoes into a cloud,
almost able to offer a home to the Holy One,

who doesn't seem to mind being
wholly devoted to dust.

The Last Two Lines of a Blessing

It didn't happen suddenly,
        the way he slipped beyond, but I

must have missed the signs, have misread the signs, didn't realize
        how few clear moons remained. First, it was that

afternoon at the burger counter, he asked if
        we could order while his food grew cold in front of him. I

held his hand afterward as he stepped
        into the car and out

of the familiar comforts of
        a worn-out way of knowing, no longer my

father, but still my father, you know? Still a blessed trinity of body
        soul & spirit. So many goodbyes, so much softness in their wake. I

help him finish sentences, chop dill, walk the dog. We would
        all call this love, wouldn't we? Enough to break

the bad habits of the heart that prefer control over reality, that harden into
        tombstones. Instead, we learn to let surrender blossom,

                                        & blossom.

Beating the Odds

Ask a skeptic, and they'll say *improbable*.

Ask a cynic, and they'll say *impossible*.

The odds are stacked
against us living at all.
Still, some sort of essence makes its way
into our resounding basilica-bodies—
this is not a metaphor,
we are dealing with sacred
architecture, we are clothed
in our own holy history. The heart
that stopped started again. The breath
that gathered strength
went galloping toward the future.
Someone is always
rolling the stone away.
Spirits feasting
on stolen flesh, decimated land
where high rises
of human abuse grate
the sallow sky,
have had too much to say.
But they don't have
the last word.

Ask the seer, and they'll say *miracle*.

Ask a poet, and they'll say *yes*.

I Want to Meet You Again, There Where You Are

I.
In Egypt, you're a thirty-dayer or a forty-dayer,
depending on how long you fast. Ramadan is shorter
than Lent. Americans have little patience for the holy
mathematics of abstention. We build houses for our cars
and expect the dessert to be decadent.
Unless we're on a diet or using the word "intermittent"
and once again divorcing science from the spirit.

II.
Fasting means
you have to eventually break
the fast. Otherwise it's starvation.
Fasting means
food when the moon is a bright belly
overhead. Otherwise it's famine.

Fasting means
your spirit feasts on what the body
holds already within itself, so close
to unbreakable fullness.
Fasting means
an angel or two in your bones,
the miracle of making space.

III.
This poem may be the only place you are asked
to know that inflation in Lebanon hit 123% in January.
The reporters have no fine similes or comforting
metaphors, and neither does the poet. At sunset,
the believers weep. Desperation is eating us alive.

IV.
In a compelling version of the truth,
the *dua* is a conversation

between the Lover and the Beloved
in which they both become Love.

Half-heartedness is a mask.
One way forward is to kneel in the sand, in the rubble
of what you expected your life to look like, and bow
down.

A prayer is a world
in which the light is a Bakerwoman
with loving hands.
Grant me light upon light, here
in my open palms.

The Sermonic Saxophone: A Found Sonnet

—after Barbara Holmes

Art can amplify the sacred.
On occasion, we turn our attention
to Billie's sultry torch songs and are startled,
as if the mysteries tune the message

to our own hearing, a cosmos you can almost reach
in the high notes. Ecclesial organizations want control
but cannot access what artists learned. The sacred
cannot be confined. Tongues perforated with pauses.

When Coltrane blew his horn, soul and spirit, bone and flesh,
were too alive for articulation. None of the expected characteristics.
Bill Robinson and Savion Glover rhyme.
Feet tapping is the ineffable divine among us.

God mediated through a saxophone.
How can this be? The angels pause to consider.

A Well-Guarded Love

—for L.A.

In a cottage near the woods lives a poet. She listens
to the rain when it rains, to the sun when it shines.
She might smoke cigarettes and eat shrimp and splurge
on expensive cheese. She went to a school where
where children are taught to listen to the secrets of
the colors.
She was delighted when she learned to fall back
into urdhva dhanurasana and devastated when
her mother
fell back into another galaxy. Once, she went out
into the Sahara and tried to love her body. Years later,
she sat on a balcony and told me about all the places
where it still hurt
and why. She told me that when I was born, *there was a*
dove-colored sky.

What If They Say

—after Jane Hirshfield

What if they say *we weren't looking?*
Stare out from the light of your own bones
and take one more step.

What if they say *we weren't listening?*
Shake the sands of everything you've heard
from your head
and build an island stronger than salt,
an island where wisdomkeepers and water-walkers
come to hear with the ears
of the heart.

What if they say *we couldn't stomach it?*
Let the body
do its own good work.

What if they say *we turned away?*
Away from one thing is toward another.
That is how direction works.
The sun rises, and the sun sets.

What if they are never done saying
what we would rather not have them say?

Let the dung beetles have their feast.

Let the right kind of silence

ring

out.

Mystery Light

Have we finally become a visionless people?

We confuse self-combusting debris for stars and blame everything
on our earthly enemies. Sometimes the light is nothing
more than space junk burning up in the atmosphere. Restoration

takes many forms. An eclipse is also a story of molting.
The sky-gazing continues. Sometimes the visitors tell stories
of coyotes and votives and sobriety, whose light is the same

as its ugliness. They return from the faraway camps carrying baskets,
woven with light. The light is more than skin stretched over the surface
of a galaxy. The stories are less than the future on an old man's tongue.

The earth is a house of stories and light.

Dear Andrea

—for Andrea Gibson

Remember when it used to be easy? Well, not *easy*, but easier? Okay, not *easier*, but familiar? *Familiar*? That's not it either. Remember when it used to be—what? I guess I don't know. Maybe just *remember*, and that's enough? A car, a coast, a longing bigger than a lover, even bigger than language, but that found a way to welcome both. A kite, so many moons, *everything other than I love you is small talk*, pennies, goosebumps, poems. Remember? Of course you do. Remembering is a grace that keeps grief from stealing the show.

I read about your latest treatment, about how long it took you to say yes to it. Last week, my poetry teacher said a poem should say no before it says yes, & I said my no a is musculature that allows my yes to move in freedom. No to making remembering do all the footwork. Yes to what is now, to whatever is now, even when that means the old unknowns & the new aches & many dropped stitches while trying to knit them all together. Yes to why I turn to you every time the key won't turn, the lock won't yield: you know you don't have to be tender—or grateful or playful or even alive at all—but you choose to be. Alive & all.

I had a plot in a community garden once, planted komatsuna & leeks & fire poppies. I loved it even when it was barren. Nothing really grew until I covered it with goat scat &urine-soaked straw. You get where I'm going with this? My daughter would sit with a notebook & sketch zinnias & cosmos at a neighboring plot. The rescue pigeons would huddle in the corner of their coop, & we never questioned why they deserved care. We just cared. It was all there—the shit & the wounded wings & the waiting & *pain becoming an instrument*. Then, eventually, the blossoming.

We had to leave that place, & I can't tell the story now because it's still more grief than grace as it rearranges my bones. But I can tell you that the city requires the beds to be cleared to get the deposit back. Goodbye overwintered arugula, not-yet-ready harlequin carrots, marigolds, mustard greens, a single brandywine tomato. Goodbye sunflowers, which I thanked, as old friends, while snipping them from their stalks & placing them into buckets. Thirty-eight in all. My age. I couldn't go home. I stood on the corner, waving people down, & gave every last sunflower away. When we're gone, they won't be able to talk about what's been lost because we will have already given it all away.

I marvel at

how repetitive, how pressing grief can be.

warmth tries to return, but its radiator is faulty. i have to ask for help
again. he sits through another seminar on befriending one's feelings.
they don't hold hands anymore. she can't take the pictures down.

memory rearranges itself into distorted mosaics. the colors
still speak, but the fragments refuse to birth into a form. blue
is a place & red is a time & green is a garish, misguided incarnation.

because loss is universal, i read a short story aloud to my students & cry
when the narrator's father succumbs to his diagnosis. another died
    with drawings
of butterflies taped on the wall, probably mid-prayer. *pater noster qui*
    non est.

we get on with it, as we do. paperwork & pots of tea &
    only disappearing
at respectable intervals. but then i see two people kiss at the
    baggage carousel.
or there's a birthday, a finisher's medal, a moonrise, a gifted pair
    of earrings.

grief is praise because it is the natural way love honors what it misses.
who else is ready to go down into the deep river of the soul & receive
the ceremony? bulrushes stand guard over each elegy's arrival.

on the anniversary of my latest Great Undoing, i cut a lock of my hair &
leave it on the balcony for the robins to carry off, strand by strand,
    to build
new nests. i marvel at how repetitive, how pressing living can be.

The Knowledge That Can't Be Eaten

—for Lewis Mehl-Madrona

Your grandmother's
pot of coffee
simmered on the stove.
The coffee was not
evaporating.
It was being sipped
by spirits.

Science
originally meant
knowledge,
whose sources have of long
and of late
been the subject
of much debate.
The Little Ones returned your wallet
to the driver's seat of your truck
once you knew what you needed
to know. Scientific fact.

Do we yet know
what your grandmother taught?
The mission of the healer
has nothing to do with slowing
the rate of the inevitable decline.
We are marching toward
the Divine. We are dancers
with Sun-skin beside
our own Spirit Lake.

With Hazel, why shouldn't we,
while still in good health,
while laughing under the quilt
in the small cabin of this life,
be able to announce,
now is my time to go
and then go?

It's Never Just About Dante

It was time to go six minutes ago, but we are not done talking.
My students are saying grief is a gift. They are saying

it's part of healing. One's father died the day before school started.
They called it "a tragic accident" and declined any further inquiry.

We are living with very persistent questions about death.
Another wears a locket, given to her by her Omie, who ran

from Budapest before the men in heavy boots and tanks
sent the rest of her family off to die. It's always somebody's yahrzeit.

The candles stay lit, the prayers run together like the deep river
of all souls where we still come to drink, even as we profess

our enlightened disbelief. Even when life becomes one long vigil,
some still praise the gift of being awake. I've seen them, after dark,

stacking stones on graves. I've seen them, kissing on park benches
in spite of the city-wide curfew. I see them here, writing in the margins

of their books, because the point of space is sometimes to take it,
even all of it. On page 56, a boy with bleached hair and a desperate

appetite for truth copied out, over and over, as if in a detention
in some bygone era, *is there anything underneath the pain?* His deskmate

takes out a pink highlighter, leans over, and writes in all caps:
YES: YOUR HEART.

After Much Scouring, the Cup Is Still Dirty

I.
For years, I repeated
first the pain, then the rising

and had to live my life
in that comma.

I am living my life
in that comma.

The whale has not
spit me out onto the other
side.

II.
To those who stayed twelve nights at the fire,
the white birds of the island
revealed that they were angels.
Vigils turn secrets inside out,
like pockets scattering gold.

Light a candle and see
how your thoughts wander away
from what you carry when
the bulbs are bright.

Your body is a shoreline.
Your soul is a wave.
Your spirit is a sea.

III.
We are trying to be the archers
who never miss the mark.
But we are the light-arrows,

and everything is a target.
Here, here, here, here & every is where
we are needed.

IV.

Yes to the unfinished clauses of becoming.
Yes to caw-words in the roofless house of prayer.
Yes to a life that demands everything of me.

Meditation on Language

My daughter is four. She says, across the dinner table,
you're projecting. Whose words is she parroting back?
A vulnerable teen confides in me, *I suspect my mother's*
love is transactional. Whose words is she experimenting with?
We piece together partialities on our way to a fullness of truth.

A poet writes *polyphonic fist?* on the board.
A poet's pen helps the wood sorrel and wild ramps live again.
A poet is always trying to invent
a language that cannot be co-opted,
that drafts itself out of slumber and into
fresh, into new.

A More Generous Grammar

Don't ask me my pronouns
as a way to know me.

They are grit. I am grease. There are no gears.

What is turning?

Ask me my adjectives: *deep/radical/wild.*

Ask me my verbs: *unbind/bridge/heal.*

Ask me for more names—*Lazarus/John/Light.*

Ask me for more reasons—*rising/becoming/beholding.*

Ask me about the dreams where a swallow sits at my breast.

If grammar presses you forward, if grammar refuses to yield,
try *we,* so as to re-member that you can't talk about me
without talking about you. Re-member that all speaking
is communion. Re-member that

we are wordsmithing our way into a future that is asking
to be

born.

AFTERWORD

What To Do With All This Beholding?

My first full-length collection of poems, *A Rare But Possible Condition*, was born of a promise I made to myself in a time of deep crisis: whenever I wanted to end my life, I would write about it instead. Aren't we all trying to make a promise worth keeping? Amen, I found one. I had just come out, which completely upended the structures that my life was built around, and staying alive and writing poems both seemed equally absurd to me. Luckily, I'd read and loved enough Kierkegaard and Camus to venture answering absurdity with art. I did so without knowing what would come of it. I did so without even believing I could do it. Self-assurance was a fool's enterprise.

When I reflect now on that stretch of impossible time, I can see how much of what I wrote was desperate and chaotic. I was obsessed with vultures and Shams of Tabriz, the crucifixion was the only truth, and all my concrete poems could pass as gravestones. Other poems from that period were noxiously poetic (aubades are really not my genre), so as to avoid having to feel profoundly stupid and abjectly alone. *And yet sometimes, an incomprehensible grace found me, nested magic words in my hair, and all I had to do was catch a good breeze for them to shake loose and land on the page.* (I would acknowledge those poems as co-authored, but I still don't know the names of the helpers who came to me.) All three of these kinds of poems are found in that first collection because they are all three true to the evolution of their maker, and maybe even true to The Maker. Doesn't every person of faith teeter on the edge of that kind of presumption?

When that book was finished, as the desperation receded, I assumed the promise had been fulfilled. I no longer needed to write to save my life. However, to my surprise, I found that now I needed to write in order to honor the life that I had saved. While I tend to loathe anything that has even a whiff of the prosperity gospel, I realized that I didn't just want to survive; I wanted to thrive. I recalled an anecdote that Pádraig Ó Tuama tells in his book *In the Shelter*. He was speaking with a woman and couldn't believe that, in her elderhood, she didn't have a philosophy of sorrow. For her part, she was incredulous that, at his young age, Pádraig didn't have a philosophy of joy. I, like Pádraig, continued to lean heavily into sorrow. Could joy befriend me again? Could the three of us—sorrow, joy, and me—walk as equal partners? Could resurrection be more than a one-time miracle? I made a new promise: I would write to find out. This is how *italics* started to take shape.

Over the course of a year or so, poetry became a wagon with which I could hitch myself to the Sacred Everyday (a phrase borrowed from Danusha Laméris and James Crews) and get a bumpy tour of what my previous pain had prevented me from seeing. The Sacred Everyday doesn't care what religion you are (or aren't) or what language you pray in (or don't) or what you've been conditioned to value (or despise) about yourself. Its only concern is to raise up disciples of beauty, goodness, and truth. I could feel it pulling me along. We covered a lot of ground (and heavens) together.

Admittedly, some days—or, more truthfully, nights—the wheels fell off my wagon. Everyday Sacred became everyday scared, and I had to haphazardly wordsmith the wheels back into functionality. Slowly but surely, a new pattern began to emerge: the more I wrote, the more I could stay the course. And the course did include joy, and playfulness, and the luminosity of the right words showing up at the right moment.

Of course, not all landscapes are picture postcard perfect. Light always casts shadows. What is given to me to see is not just amber flooding the rugged California coast at dusk; it's not just the self-love notes my daughter writes to herself and hangs on the wall of her bedroom. It's also endangered species and petty arguments and the shame of former selves and war. Joy without sorrow or sorrow without joy are half-truths so pernicious that we might as well call them lies, and I seek neither to deceive nor be deceived.

As a collection, *italics* started to come together after realizing that I was using so many italicized words in my poems. I was enchanted by how they could change the way I felt when I wrote them and the way experienced them as a reader. I first started playing with this dynamic after reading Joan Didion's *The Year of Magical Thinking*, and two poems in my first collection directly address the impact of italics on attention. I loved the elegance with which they stopped me in my tracks, pulled me into the world of a single word, and made me want to stay there a while. Since this collection is in many ways the story of my staying, it seemed right to see where it could lead.

Although the poems in *italics* are not as heavy as my older ones, they are still engaged in reckoning: what to do with all this beholding? As a poet (and human being), I am not satisfied with being merely a spectator of scenes. I can only claim to know insofar as I do: the aim is participation. A poem that stays on the page is incomplete. A poet has to look at the world and see more. *italics* is a book for people, like me, who know that if we want a better world, we have to make it. *What we need has to be made*. Where should we start?

ACKNOWLEDGMENTS

I thank the following publications for publishing poems from this collection:

"After Much Scouring, the Cup Is Still Dirty": *Porkbelly Press*

"I marvel at": *Braided Way Magazine*

"I Want to Meet You Again, There Where You Are": *Pensive: An International Journal of Spirituality and the Arts*

"If the Point Were to Tell It Straight, Not Slant": *Rattle Poetry*

"In the Hills": *Clepsydra Magazine*

"It's Never Just About Dante": *Exsolutas Press*

"Love Is a School of Fire": *Pensive: An International Journal of Spirituality and the Arts*

"Menstruation Haibun at Sinkyone Wilderness State Park": *Willows Wept Review*

"Mystery Light": *Rattle Poetry*

"Prairie Haibun: Between Two Storms": *Untenured*

"Souvenirs": *Red Noise Collective*

"The Sermonic Saxophone: A Found Sonnet": *Local Gems Poetry Press*

"The Students Teach Me What to Write": *The Auto-Ethnographer: A Literary and Arts Magazine*

"Two California Condors Stage a Takeover of the Baltimore Catechism, Volume 2, Lessons 1-7": *Untenured*

"What's My Line, Part One: A Friday Afternoon": *Driftwood Press*

ABOUT THE AUTHOR

Alison Davis is an award-winning educator, author, artist, and activist living in Northern California. She writes more to ponder than to postulate, more to wonder than prove. As an educator, Alison is devoted to the art of initiation: how can we learn to affirm that whatever befalls us is for us so that we can belong more freely and wholly to ... everything? This deep affirmation is what brings her to the classroom, whether it takes the form of a school, a forest, a hospital wing, a prison rec room, a house of prayer, a yoga studio, or a mountaintop.

Alison's work has been featured in numerous literary and scholarly publications, including *Rattle Poetry, The Sun Magazine, Pensive: A Global Journal of Spirituality and the Arts, Braided Way, Research Bulletin*, and *SAUTI: Stanford Journal of African Studies*, as well as in popular media around the world, including the *New York Times, CNN, Channel 4, Le Temps*, and *Le Tube*. Alison is the author of the book *A Rare But Possible Condition* and the chapbook *Wild Canvas*.

www.ingramcontent.com/pod-product-compliance
Lightning Source LLC
LaVergne TN
LVHW041123150826
845673LV00007B/2171

* 9 7 8 1 9 6 1 7 4 1 3 0 0 *